Discovering
Early California
Afro-Latino Presence

Damany M. Fisher

Heyday, Berkeley, California

This pamphlet was supported by the National Park Service's Challenge Cost Share Program
and the Juan Bautista de Anza National Historic Trail. The points of view presented in this
pamphlet are those of the author and do not necessarily represent the position of the Depart-
ment of the Interior.

In 1990, Congress established the Juan Bautista de Anza National Historic Trail as part of the
National Trails System. The trail commemorates, protects, marks, and interprets the route that
Anza traveled during 1775 and 1776 from Sonora, Mexico, to take settlers to present-day San
Francisco, California, to establish a mission and presidio. The twelve-hundred-mile trail in the
United States traverses from Nogales, Arizona, to San Francisco. Another six hundred miles
of the historic route travel through the states of Sinaloa and Sonora, Mexico. Today, you may
travel portions of the trail by car, foot, horse, bicycle, or train.

Juan Bautista de Anza National Historic Trail

Cover Art: Edward Vischer, *A California Magnate in His Home*, 1865. Courtesy of The Bancroft
    Library, University of California, BANC PIC 19xx.039:33—FR
Design: Rebecca LeGates
Printed by Medius Corporation, San Jose, California

Orders, inquiries, and correspondence should be addressed to:
    Heyday
    P. O. Box 9145, Berkeley, CA 94709
    (510) 549-3564, Fax (510) 549-1889
    www.heydaybooks.com

10 9 8 7 6 5 4 3 2 1

Introduction

Among the earliest non-indigenous residents of California were hundreds of people of African background who descended from slaves taken to Mexico during the fifteenth and sixteenth centuries. These *Afro-Latinos*, as they have come be called, helped shape the character of California much as Puritans shaped the character of New England. They blazed trails and established towns and ranches that grew into major cities, such as Los Angeles, San Diego, Monterey, and San Jose. Several amassed considerable fortunes and acquired high-ranking positions in the military and government.

Why isn't the African contribution to early California better known? Perhaps the absence of Afro-Latinos in public consciousness can be attributed to popular images rendered by the nineteenth-century European artists who traveled throughout California to study and report on the various peoples and cultures. Some of their descriptions of Spanish-speaking Californians, or Californios, were quite idealistic and not entirely accurate. Take for instance

Charles Christian Nahl (American, born Germany, 1818–1878), *The Fandango*, 1873. This image portrays a romantic view of Californios in the nineteenth century. Oil on canvas, 72 x 108 inches. Crocker Art Museum, E. B. Crocker Collection, 1872.386. Courtesy of Crocker Art Museum.

1

the 1873 painting *Fandango*, by artist Charles Christian Nahl. The painting presents a romanticized view of life on a California rancho: a place where people lived free of care and spent the majority of their time in leisure and comfort. Nahl and others often showed Californios displaying their remarkable horsemanship in rodeos or performing traditional dances like the *fandango* and the *contradanza*.

But can the history of Spanish-speaking Californians be summed up in a description of a fandango? A deeper look into the history of pre–Gold Rush California reveals that Spanish-speaking Californians developed a society that was just as complex as any that existed in the United States. But unlike the United States, where people of different ethnic and racial backgrounds were largely segregated, early nineteenth-century California was a place where Afro-Latino, mestizo, European, and Indian lived side by side and frequently intermarried. Of course, these relationships were not always harmonious. Thousands of Native Americans, for example, faced abuse and exploitation in California missions and often were forced to work for the Spanish. Nevertheless, it was a much more egalitarian society than Mexico, where special rights and privileges were reserved to Spaniards of "pure blood." In California, Afro-Latinos had greater social, economic, and political opportunities, some acquiring vast tracts of land or serving as military officers or government officials. By contrast, most African Americans in the United States in the eighteenth and early nineteenth century were enslaved. Even free African Americans enjoyed few, if any, legal rights.

Arrival of Cortés in Mexico, followed by his black servant (Moorish soldier known variously as Estevan, Estevanico, and Esteban) and preceded by La Malinche, his mistress and translator. Sixteenth-century Codex Azcatitlan. Bibliotheque Nationale, Paris, France, Ms mexicains no. 59–94. Photo credit: Snark/Art Resource, NY.

Africans in Mexico

Few students of American history know that the first Africans in North America accompanied Spanish conquistadors as early as the sixteenth century. For example, Juan Garrido, a black soldier, served under Hernán Cortés in the defeat of the Aztec empire in 1521. Five years later, Luis Vásquez de Ayllón took one hundred African slaves to present-day Georgetown, South Carolina, in an unsuccessful attempt to build a Spanish settlement there. African slaves were also among those who joined Hernando de Soto on an expedition from Florida to the Mississippi River in 1536. Similarly, in 1539 Francisco Vásquez de Coronado led an exploratory mission that also included Africans or people of African descent to the area that includes the modern states of Arizona, New Mexico, and Texas. That same year, Estevan, a black Muslim, traveled with Alvar Núñez Cabeza de Vaca from Texas to Sinaloa. African laborers contributed significantly to the construction of St. Augustine, Florida, in 1565—the oldest city in the United States. Thus, long before the first successful English settlement in Jamestown, Virginia, Afro-Latinos had not only explored but resided in what is now the United States of America.

Most Afro-Latinos in the sixteenth and seventeenth centuries were slaves. They were sent to work in Spanish colonies like Mexico, Hispaniola, Cuba, Puerto Rico, Colombia, and Peru. Between 1518 and 1870, Spanish America imported over 1.5 million enslaved Africans, mostly through Cuba and South America.

The conquest of Mexico by the Spanish conquistador Hernán Cortés (1485–1547): the departure in 1518. African-born explorer Juan Garrido is pictured at far left. Sixteenth-century manuscript. Bibliothèque Nationale, Paris, France. Photo credit: Scala/White Images/Art Resource, NY.

Spain introduced African slaves into Mexico because, in part, the decline of the indigenous Mexican population during the sixteenth century had led to a labor shortage: the combination of Spanish brutality and disease had decimated Mexico's Indian population. As the population declined, the colonial economy evolved. Spain needed laborers to work in colonial silver mines, cultivate sugar cane, produce textiles, and work on cattle ranches. Several members of the Spanish clergy, most notably Bartolomé de las Casas, protested the poor treatment of Indians and suggested that Africans—whom they considered infidels and culturally inferior—be used as slaves instead.

Perhaps as many as fifty thousand Africans had been sent to Mexico before 1580 (many to Spain initially, then to Mexico). Between 1580 and 1670, roughly one hundred thousand slaves, mostly Africans, were taken to Mexico. Vera Cruz, a town on Mexico's Caribbean coast, was a frequent destination for slave traders. Enslaved Africans were sent from Vera Cruz and other towns to work as servants and laborers throughout the Spanish colonies. By 1645 Mexico had a slave population of eighty thousand.

Apart from being used on the sugar plantations, a substantial number of enslaved Africans worked in the cities as domestics and personal servants. Others worked as teamsters, gilders, meat cutters, dyers, blacksmith's helpers, and so on. During the seventeenth century, slaves were used as soldiers in Vera Cruz. In 1621 there were sixty-four slaves who worked with the military in some capacity, mostly as manual laborers. Blacks in Colima, Huatulco, Acapulco, and Oaxaca worked on cacao plantations and ranches.

Black labor was considered particularly valuable in Mexico's mining districts; Spanish colonists believed that Indians were physically incapable of performing that type of work well. By 1597, enslaved Africans represented

Clothing Styles, Lima, Peru, 1748: African slaves working as domestic servants in colonial Peru. After the conquest of the Inca Empire in 1532, Spain imported thousands of African slaves. Most of them were concentrated in and around Lima, clearing land and building roads and buildings. Most women slaves performed highly valued domestic tasks like cooking and laundering. From www.slaveryimages.org, sponsored by the Virginia Foundation for the Humanities and the University of Virginia Library, JCB_07822-4.

16 percent of a total workforce comprising Indians and Africans. These mining areas included Zultepec, Temascaltepec, Guanajuato, Tlalpuxagua, Zacualpa, Pachuca, Ocumatlan, Cuautla, Taxco, and Zacatecas. Like the Indians, enslaved Africans met with the cruelty of Spanish overseers. As a matter of fact, demand for more slaves was ongoing because slaves were routinely worked to death in Mexico's mines and fields.

Theodore de Bry (1528–1598): "After exterminating the indigenous population in Hispaniola (Haiti) the Spanish bring in African slaves from Guinea to exploit the mineral wealth of the country," 1595. This image is an illustration for Girolamo Benzoni's *Americae*, part V; de Bry, a Flemish engraver, never himself traveled to the Americas. Color engraving. Kunstbibliothek, Staatliche Museen, Berlin, Germany. Photo by Knud Petersen, courtesy of Bildarchiv Preussischer Kulturbesitz/Art Resource, NY.

Map of New Spain showing solar eclipse, Mission San Diego, 1688; "Por orden de S.M.N. el So. Virrey de la Nueva España: Do. Gaspar de la Cerda Silva y Mendoza, se delinio sobre las Provincias que tanto mal Recibieron por que se oscurecio el sol y uvo mucho temor y los Indios. Facieron muchos descatos y mal porque no uvo cosechas." Courtesy of The Bancroft Library, University of California, Map G 04411 B1 1688 P6 Case A.

Felipe Guaman Poma de Ayala: "How the Spaniards Abuse Their African Slaves," 1600–1615, Peru, from *El primer nueva coronica y buen gobierno*, a critique of Spanish colonial rule addressed to King Philip III of Spain. From www.slaveryimages.org, sponsored by the Virginia Foundation for the Humanities and the University of Virginia Library, Guaman925.

Spain's legal code, the *Siete Partidas*, gave slaves certain rights unimaginable in the British colonies and in the United States. For instance, if a slave could find wealthy godparents for her children she could often obtain freedom for the children with a small payment—a few pesos—to the master. Slaves were permitted to work on Sundays and holidays and apply their earnings toward their freedom. Sometimes clergymen negotiated favorable terms for slaves to purchase their freedom. A slave raped by a master could sue for her freedom. Many slaves were emancipated upon the death of a master or mistress, or in recognition of loyal service. In effect, it was easier under Spanish law than other codes for slave-masters to free their slaves.

By the eighteenth century, free blacks outnumbered slaves in Mexico and had a noticeable presence in Mexico City, Puebla, and Vera Cruz. Others were dispersed throughout the countryside and mining centers like Culiacán, Sinaloa, and Zacatecas.

Although the Spanish showed less hostility toward free blacks than the English in colonies in North America and the Caribbean, free blacks in Mexico—especially those in Mexico City and Puebla—faced many obstacles. Some cities passed laws that kept them from obtaining land and barred them from certain skilled professions. This may explain why some free blacks moved into the frontier regions of Mexico, where they encountered much less discrimination. By the eighteenth century, free black communities had sprung up in several towns and districts northeast of Mexico City, in places like Rosario (now El Rosario), Cosala, Villa Sinaloa (now Sinaloa de Leyva), Durango (now Victoria de Durango), Culiacán (now Culiacán Rosales), Parral (now Hidalgo del Parral), and Horcasitas. The shortage of Spanish settlers in these remote areas provided opportunities for Afro-Latinos to serve in the military and work in traditionally restricted professions, like tailoring. Mazatlán de los Mulatos was established in 1576 by a group of free blacks who were granted land in the area as recompense for escorting travelers to Culiacán. By 1760, roughly one thousand Afro-Latinos lived in the town's presidio, all of them soldiers charged with protecting the Port of Mazatlán. A few of these soldiers relocated to the Bay of Mazatlán and established a small fishing community around 1800. By the late eighteenth century, Mazatlán and other peripheral towns included Afro-Latino soldiers, merchants, artisans, priests, mayors, councilmen, ranchers, and farmers.

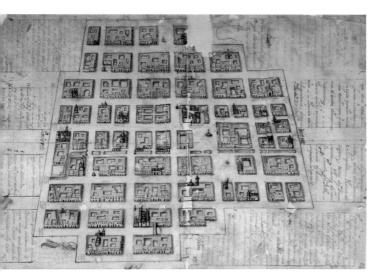

Mexico City, 1720. This map was produced by the city government to aid officials in improving garbage collection. Antonio Alvarez, cartographer. Miguel Rivera, creator. Courtesy of World Digital Library.

Anonymous, eighteenth century: *Human Races (Las Castas)*. To maintain social hierarchy in the Americas, Spanish officials placed the colonial population into various racial groups, or *castas*—for example, *mestizo* (indigenous and European), *mulato* (African and European), and *lobo* (American native and African). These paintings reveal not only the presence of Africans in Spanish colonial society, but also the degree to which Africans mixed into the general population. The 1790 census in California identified a significant number of residents as "mulato." Oil on canvas, 1.04 x 1.48 m. Museo Nacional del Virreinato, Tepotzotlan, Mexico. Photo Credit: Schalkwijk/Art Resource, NY

The Juan Bautista de Anza Expedition and Afro-Latino Settlement in California

So how did Afro-Latinos eventually find their way to modern-day California? *Answer:* The Juan Bautista de Anza Expedition. Originally established to supply Alta California missions and block other European nations from gaining control of the area, the Anza trail made possible the migration of free blacks and mestizos to Spain's northernmost province. Like many immigrants today, Afro-Latinos pursued the promise of better lives for themselves and their families in California.

In 1773 Juan Bautista de Anza, captain of the small Presidio of Tubac in Sonora (now southern Arizona), received permission from Antonio María Bucareli y Ursúa, viceroy of New Spain, to find an overland route from Sonora to northern California. In January of 1774 Captain Anza, Father Francisco Garcés, a small group of soldiers and servants, and a herd of about two hundred cattle and pack animals left Tubac to open the new supply route. By the end of March, Anza and part of his expedition had arrived at Mission San Gabriel (near what is now the city of Los Angeles). An overland route to Alta California was now available for use in transporting supplies and colonists to the outermost reaches of northern New Spain. For his efforts, the Spanish Crown promoted Anza to lieutenant colonel.

In 1773, Juan Bautista de Anza, captain of the small Presidio of Tubac in Sonora (now southern Arizona) was commissioned by the Spanish Crown to find an overland route from Mexico's mainland to California. Found with the assistance of the Yuma Indians, Anza's overland route enabled Spain to expand its influence over its northern province. National Park Service photo.

Eager to follow up on his initial success, Anza arrived in Mexico City in November of 1774 to seek permission to lead another expedition to California. This time, Anza wanted to take with him not only a military garrison but dozens of families. His plan met with little opposition from Spanish officials and he soon set out to recruit volunteers. He traveled

throughout northwestern Mexico and appealed to residents of Culiacán, Villa
Sinaloa, Altar, Horcasitas, and other towns to join him. These and other towns
in Mexico's northwest supplied California with many of its earliest settlers.

Of the soldiers and settlers that Anza recruited to migrate to Alta California, Afro-Latinos made up a significant portion. Felipe Santiago Tapia, who
would, along with his sons, become a large-scale rancher in southern California, joined Anza on this second expedition. Also included was Santiago de
la Cruz Pico, who became patriarch to one of the most powerful families in
Mexican-era California. His son, José María Pico, just seven years old at the
time of the expedition, was the father of Andrés Pico and future California
Governor Pío Pico.

After purchasing livestock and supplies in various Mexican towns, Anza
and his volunteers traveled north to Tubac. By the time the expedition left
Tubac on October 23, 1775, it had grown to three hundred people. For nearly
five months they traveled by horseback, mule, and on foot, arriving at the
presidio in Monterey on March 10, 1776. That year the San Francisco presidio
was built, and by the early part of 1777 an agricultural colony had been established at San Jose. The Anza colonists had not only doubled the number of settlers in California; they had greatly increased the number of cattle and horses.

Another less known but important member of the expedition was María
Feliciana Arballo. Arballo was a widow who pleaded with Anza to allow her
and her two daughters—María Tomasa Gutiérrez and María Eustaquia—to

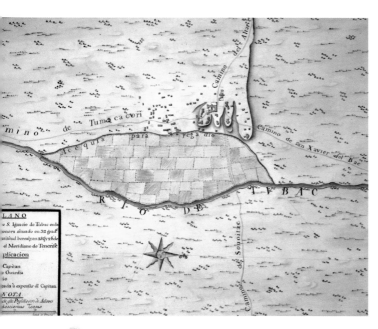

Joseph de Urrutia, "Plano del Presidio de Tubac en la provincia de Sonora," 1766-67. Tubac was established in 1752 and was the first Spanish colonial garrison in Arizona. Juan Bautista de Anza was stationed there from 1760 to 1776. Courtesy of The British Library, Additional MS. 17,662.h.

travel with him to San Francisco. According to official marriage records from the Cathedral of Culiacán, Arballo was described as a "mulata libre," or a free black woman. When, on the evening of December 17, 1775, the three parties

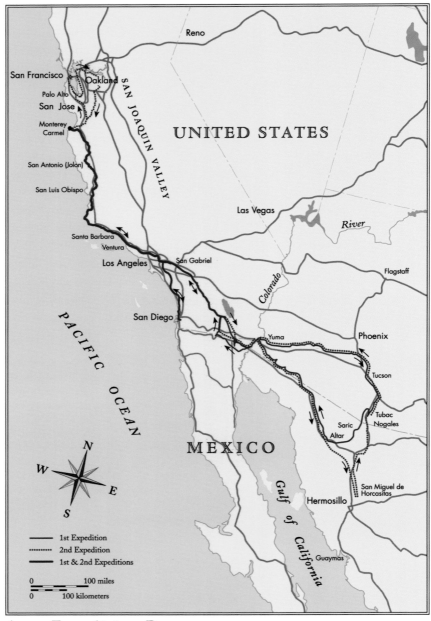

Anza Expedition Routes

into which Anza had divided the expedition reunited at San Sebastian, east of San Diego near the Salton Sea, Father Pedro Font mentioned her in his journal:

> At night, with the joy at the arrival of all the people, they held a fandango here. It was somewhat discordant, and a very bold widow who came with the expedition sang some verses which were not at all nice, applauded and cheered by all the crowd. For this reason the man to whom she came attached became angry and punished her. The commander, hearing of this, sallied forth from his tent and reprimanded the man because he was chastising her. I said to him, "Leave him alone, Sir, he is doing just right," but he replied, "No, Father, I cannot permit such excesses when I am present." He guarded against this excess, indeed, but not against the scandal of the fandango, which lasted until very late.

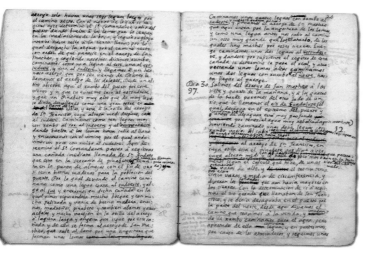

Pages from Pedro Font's diary chronicling the 1775-76 Anza expedition. This entry is for March 29, 1776. Courtesy of The Bancroft Library, University of California, BANC MSS M-M 1724 pgs. 23v–24r.

María Feliciana Arballo left the Anza expedition once it reached San Gabriel. There, she married Juan Francisco López, a native of Baja California who was serving as a member of the mission guard. Her daughters and grandchildren would later gain enormous status by marrying into prominent Californio families. María Eustaquia, for instance, married José María Pico and they became the parents of Pío Pico, the last Mexican governor of California.

Why did these families decide to risk their lives and move to California? Perhaps one reason was the flood of 1770, which had left hundreds homeless, particularly in Sinaloa and southern Sonora. Some families had already moved to other towns following the flood. The Pico family, for instance, had originally come from Xavier de Cabazán (now Cabazán), in Sinaloa, but Anza recruited them at San Miguel de Horcasitas Presidio, in Sonora.

Financial reasons, too, may have compelled Afro-Latinos to undertake the move. Silver and gold production had declined sharply in Sonoran and Sinaloan towns. Mines often flooded, and they suffered from inadequate drainage. Towns like Alamos, Rosario, and Cosala were known to be very poor by the late eighteenth century. Not surprisingly, Anza managed to find several volunteers in this area.

The success of Anza's 1775-76 expedition convinced Spanish officials that the overland route provided the best opportunity to settle Alta California and fortify their control over the region. In 1781 another expedition of soldiers and settlers set out for California, this time under the leadership of Fernando de Rivera y Moncada. This led to the settlement of Los Angeles and Santa Barbara. Like Anza, Rivera recruited Afro-Latino families, from Loreto, in Baja California, and Sonora and Sinaloa. Among those who traveled with

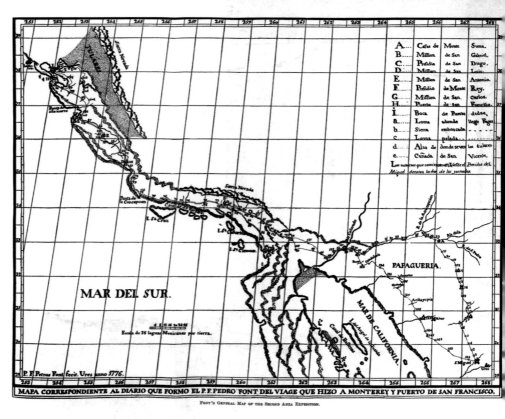

Above and opposite: Pedro Font, Maps of Anza's route, 1776. Courtesy of the National Park Service.

Rivera were <u>José Manuel Pérez Nieto</u>, a mulatto soldier who helped found Los Angeles, and Luis Quintero, a mulatto tailor whose family were among the earliest residents of Santa Barbara.

By 1790 Afro-Latinos made up nearly 20 percent of California's population. That means that one out of every five residents in California was known to be of African background! The concept of "race" had far less importance in California than in the United States. While European-born Spaniards controlled California society, Afro-Latinos and mestizos did manage to gain political and economic influence during the Spanish and Mexican periods of California history.

Prominent Afro-Latino Families in California

Calisornia gave many Afro-Latinos a chance to live the type of life they could not have imagined back in Mexico. Below are some brief biographical narratives of prominent Afro-Latino families: the Brioneses, the Nietos, the Picos, and the Tapias.

THE BRIONES FAMILY

In 1771 Vicente Briones and his son Marcos José Briones migrated to California from Mexico. The elder Briones had been a soldier sent to serve at the presidio in San Francisco and would later serve a brief stint as commissioner at Branciforte (modern-day Santa Cruz), in 1812.

Vicente's daughter Juana Briones, whose mother and grandparents arrived in California with the Anza Expedition in 1776, became a fixture in Yerba Buena (present-day San Francisco) during the nineteenth century. She developed a reputation for being a savvy businesswoman and landowner as well as a humanitarian and healer. In 1820 she married a garrison corporal at the presidio named Apolinario Miranda. Their marriage ended in divorce and Briones, along with her eight children, moved into an adobe house in Yerba Buena, where she set up a practice as a healer. She also supported herself by

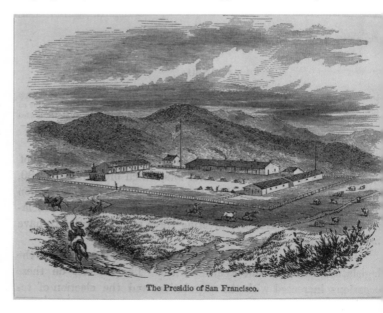

Unknown artist. *The Presidio of San Francisco, 1849.* Robert B. Honeyman, Jr. Collection of Early Californian and Western American Pictorial Material. Courtesy of The Bancroft Library, University of California, BANC PIC 1963.002:0625:01—A

The Presidio of San Francisco.

This image is believed to be of Juana Briones, by a descendant of hers. Briones, a woman of mixed African, European, and indigenous heritage, arrived in California with her parents on the Anza expedition of 1776. National Park Service, Point Reyes National Seashore Archives.

selling milk and vegetables at the presidio. Briones later purchased a 4400-acre parcel named Rancho la Purísima Concepcion in present-day Santa Clara County. Juana Briones died in 1889. The house located on the property still stands and efforts are underway to preserve it. It is listed on the California State Register as California Historical Landmark No. 524.

Juana Briones's brother Gregorio Briones received, in 1846, an 8900-acre land grant that he named Rancho las Baulinas. It was located in what is now Marin County, near the town of Bolinas. Gregorio later served as *alcalde* (mayor) of Contra Costa, San Mateo, and Sonoma. Another brother, Felipe Santiago Briones, served on the council of Pueblo San Jose in 1820.

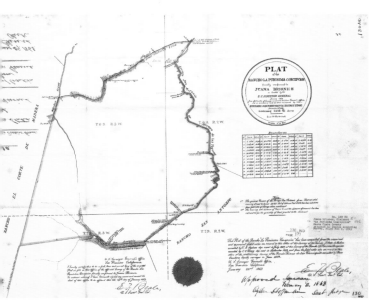

Plat of the Rancho la Purísima Concepción. Located in present-day Santa Clara County, the 4400-acre Rancho la Purísima Concepción was owned by Juana Briones. The ranch house still exists and is listed as California State Landmark No. 524. Courtesy of The Bancroft Library, University of California, Berkeley, Land Case Maps Collection, Map E-281.

THE NIETO FAMILY

José Manuel Pérez Nieto arrived in Alta California in 1769. Nieto was one of the leather-jacket soldiers in Gaspar de Portolá's expedition from Mexico. He served for a brief period at the presidio at Monterey. He married María Teresa Morillo, a mestiza, after returning to Mexico in 1778 and was soon reassigned to the military guard that escorted the group of *pobladores* that eventually founded the pueblo at Los Angeles in 1781. Three years later, he petitioned Governor Pedro Fages for permission to keep his cattle and horses at a place called La Sanja (or La Zanja), roughly nine miles from Mission San Gabriel. Fages agreed to Nieto's request:

José Cardero (1768–after 1800), *Presidio de Monterey*, c. 1791. Several of Monterey's earliest residents were Afro-Latinos who arrived with the Anza expedition in March of 1776. By 1790, roughly 18 percent of Monterey's population was Afro-Latino. Robert B. Honeyman, Jr. Collection of Early Californian and Western American Pictorial Material. Courtesy of The Bancroft Library, University of California, BANC PIC 1963.002:1310—FR

Map of Los Angeles in 1794. Archivo General de Indias, Seville, Spain. Photo Credit: Scala/Art Resource, NY.

San Gabriel, October 21, 1784

I grant the petitioner the permission of having the bovine stock and horses at the place of La Sanja, or its environs; provided no harm is done to the Mission San Gabriel nor to the Pagan Indians of its environs in any manner whatsoever; and that he must have someone to watch it, and to go and sleep at the aforementioned Pueblo.

—Pedro Fages

Altogether, the Nieto grant came to around 300,000 acres. After several conflicts with Mission San Gabriel, whose property overlapped his grant, Nieto's holdings were reduced to roughly 158,000 acres. Rancho Los Nietos, as it came to be called, included the modern cities of Long Beach, Huntington Beach, Norwalk, Downey, and all the intermediate districts. At the time of his

Ferdinand Deppe, Mission San Gabriel in 1832. Courtesy of the Santa Barbara Mission Archive Library.

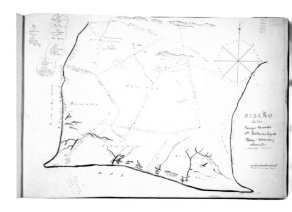

"Rancho los Nietos." The 158,000-acre Rancho los Nietos belonged to Manuel Nieto, an Afro-Latino soldier who served under Gaspar de Portolá and became one of the wealthiest landowners in southern California. In 1833 Nieto's heirs divided the original grant into six great ranchos—Los Alamitos, Los Cerritos, Los Coyotes, Las Bolsas, Palo Alto, and Santa Gertrudes—which laid the foundation for the modern cities of Long Beach, Huntington Beach, Norwalk, and Downey, and the intermediate districts. Courtesy of Charles E. Young Research Library Special Collections, University of California, Los Angeles.

death in 1804, Manuel Nieto's property and large herds of horses and "black cattle" made him the wealthiest man in California.

Upon his death, Nieto's four children, Juan José, Manuela, Antonio María, and José Antonio, inherited their father's estate. In 1833, Nieto's heirs divided the original grant into six great ranchos—Los Alamitos, Los Cerritos, Los Coyotes, Las Bolsas, Palo Alto, and Santa Gertrudes.

THE PICO FAMILY

The Picos became one of the wealthiest and most politically influential families in early California. In 1775, thirty-eight-year-old Santiago de la Cruz Pico, along with his wife, María Jacinta Bastida, and children left their home in Sinaloa and took part in the 1775-76 Anza expedition. Pico's oldest son, José María Pico, served in the military. In 1790, José María married then eighteen-year-old María Eustaquia Gutiérrez, who had traveled with her mother, María Feliciana Arballo, in the same Anza expedition. Two of their sons, Pío de Jesús and Andrés, came to be among the most accomplished of all Afro-Latinos in California.

Like their father and uncles, Andrés and Pío de Jesús Pico made the most of the opportunities available to young California-born men after 1821, when Spanish rule ended in Mexico. The rise of Andrés and Pío was due, in part, to the development of territorial assemblies such as the Diputación. Andrés used his influence to acquire large landholdings and served briefly as a delegate to Mexico City. Andrés was also a commander of the *abajeños* (lowlanders, or southern Californians), a group that favored moving the capital from Monterey to Los Angeles. In December 1846, during the Mexican-American War, Andrés led Mexican forces in defeat of the Americans at the Battle of

Above: Edward Vischer, *A California Magnate in His Home*, 1865. Andrés Pico, the younger brother of California Governor Pío Pico, became a successful ranchero and served briefly as a delegate to Mexico City, and later in the California legislature. A brilliant military strategist, in 1846 he led Mexican forces to victory at the Battle of San Pasqual. Courtesy of The Bancroft Library, University of California, BANC PIC 19xx.039:33—FR

eneral Don Andrés Pico, 1878. Photograph
 V. Wolfenstein. Courtesy of The Bancroft
brary, University of California, Portrait
ollection, Pico, Andres, 1810–1876.

San Pasqual. One month later, in January 1847, he was forced to surrender to John C. Frémont. After California became a territory of the United States, Andrés served briefly as a member of the state legislature. His wife, Catarina Moreno, was the granddaughter of José and María Guadalupe Moreno, two Afro-Latino founders of the pueblo of Los Angeles.

Pío de Jesús Pico was born on May 5, 1801, at the mission at San Gabriel, the fourth

Governor Pío Pico. Courtesy of The Bancroft Library, University of California, Portrait Collection, Pico, Pío, 1801–1894.

Like his brother Andrés, Pío de Jesús Pico rose through the ranks of California politics as a member of the Diputación. In 1845 he became the last governor of California under Mexican rule. Whittier National Trust and Savings Bank Collection, Whittier Public Library, Box B WNTSB 073. Courtesy of Whittier Public Library.

Family of Pío Pico, ca. 1850. Courtesy of San Diego History Center.

Pío Pico's mansion, 1937. In 1850, Pío Pico purchased 8,891 acres in present-day Whittier from the heirs of Juan Crispin Perez and named the land El Ranchito. In 1867 massive floods destroyed many of El Ranchito's original buildings. In 1870 Pico built another house (seen in this photograph) that would become known as one of the finest hotels in the Southwest. Whittier Historical Photograph Collection, Whittier Public Library, WHPC PIC-004. Courtesy of Whittier Public Library.

child of José María Pico and his wife, María. Like his brother Andrés, Pío de Jesús Pico rose through the ranks of California politics as a member of the Diputación. He made his greatest impact as a leader of rebellious Californios who challenged the policies of Mexican governors such as Manuel Victoria and Manuel Micheltorena. Pico succeeded both men as governor after their departures from California. As governor, Pico issued land grants totaling hundreds of thousands of acres to Mexican and American applicants alike. He was the last governor (1845-46) of California under Mexican rule.

As a young man Pico, like other Californios, was inspired by the liberal ideas of the Mexican constitution of 1824. Most of these men were born in California and felt a strong sense of connection and loyalty to their homeland. Rejecting the preeminence of military rule in California, these young Californios sought fundamental changes to the region's economic and political institutions, including a provincial constitution and the establishment of public schools. Pico emerged as one of the leading reformers. In his 1877 narrative, Pico recalled his experience working as secretary to Captain Don Pablo de la Portilla, attorney general for Alta California. Together they traveled to Los Angeles to confront Señor Bringas, a Mexican businessman accused of embezzling government funds. When Portilla confronted Bringas with these charges, Bringas informed him that he refused to answer any questions except in the presence of a civil authority. "This really impressed me profoundly," said Pico, "because we considered a captain a personage of high rank and distinction." Bringas's words had such a profound impact on the young Pico that the latter defied orders from the commandant of San Diego and was subsequently arrested. This experience affirmed his conviction that "the citizens were the nation and that no military was superior to us."

THE TAPIA FAMILY

Felipe Santiago Tapia, an Afro-Latino soldier from Culiacán, Sinaloa, arrived in California around 1775 with the first Anza expedition. Juana María Hernández, Tapia's first wife and the mother of his first nine children, died shortly thereafter. By 1776, Tapia was remarried to Juana María Cárdenas, with whom he fathered five more children, all born at the mission at Santa Clara. Tapia was also stationed at the presidio at San Francisco and stayed in California until his death in 1811 at Mission San Gabriel.

José Bartolomé Tapia, the oldest son of Felipe and his first wife, Juana, became the recipient of Rancho Topanga Malibu Sequit, a 31,315-acre land grant located along the ocean, west of present-day Los Angeles. José Bartolomé Tapia served as *mayordomo*—a civilian supervisory post—at San Luis

Henry Miller, Mission San Luis Obispo, ca. 1856. In 1790 José Bartolomé Tapia, an Afro-Latino, served as *mayordomo* at San Luis Obispo (founded by Father Junípero Serra in 1772). Courtesy of The Bancroft Library, University of California.

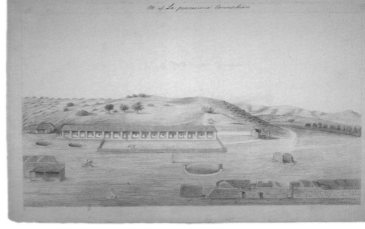

Henry Miller, Mission la Purísima Concepción, ca. 1856. Courtesy of The Bancroft Library, University of California.

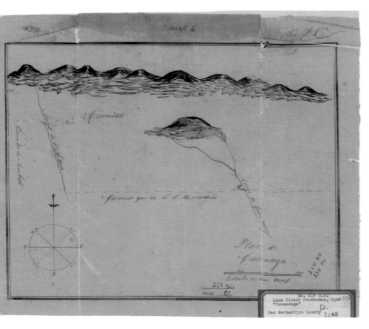

Plan of Rancho Cucamonga. Tiburcio Tapia, who served in the provincial legislature, as mayor of Los Angeles, and as a judge, purchased this 13,045-acre rancho east of present-day Los Angeles. Today, hundreds of thousands live in Rancho Cucamonga and surrounding communities. Courtesy of The Bancroft Library, University of California, Berkeley, Land Case Maps Collection, Map D-1248.

aría Merced Tapia, daughter of Tibur- Tapia. Courtesy of the Seaver Center Western History Research, Los Ange- County Museum of Natural History.

Obispo in 1790. The post of mayordomo was probably the best civilian job in California during the colonial regime, for both payment and prestige, exceeded only by the occupation of ranchero in the late colonial period.

José Bartolomé's son Tiburcio Tapia served as a soldier at Santa Barbara before assuming duties as corporal of La Purísima Mission (present-day Lompoc). In 1824, at La Purísima, Tiburcio was forced to surrender the mission temporarily to Chumash Indians who had revolted against Mexican officials.

In 1839 Tiburcio was granted 13,045 acres by Governor Juan Bautista Alvarado in an area east of Los Angeles called "Cucamonga." Using Indian labor, Tapia built an adobe home on Red Hill and raised herds of cattle. He later established a successful winery. Tapia's daughter María Merced Tapia de Prudhomme and her husband, Leon Victor Prudhomme, sold the Cucamonga Rancho in 1858 to former cattle driver John Rains.

By the 1840s Tiburcio Tapia was also politically connected and would serve as a member of the provincial legislature, a three-term mayor of Los Angeles, and a judge. One observer described him as someone who "by honorable and industrious labor had amassed so much of this world's goods as to make him one of the wealthiest inhabitants of the place [California]."

The daughters of Felipe and José Bartolomé Tapia married into prominent families, strengthening and spreading their African heritage to families such as the Brioneses and Nietos. These close relationships existed among a number of Afro-Latino families who later rose to prominence in Mexican-ruled California.

Los Angeles, ca. 1850s. Los Angeles was established as a small agricultural community nine miles southwest of Mission San Gabriel. The majority of the pueblo's founders were from Sinaloa and roughly half of these were Afro-Latino. Francisco Reyes, an Afro-Latino soldier, served as *alcalde* (chief administrative and judicial officer) of the pueblo in the 1790s. Robert B. Honeyman, Jr. Collection of Early Californian and Western American Pictorial Material. Courtesy of The Bancroft Library, University of California, BANC PIC 1963.002:0478:10—A

The United States, Manifest Destiny, and the Decline of Afro-Latino Influence in California

In the 1840s, several leading Californios began expressing some concern, if not apprehension, over the growing American presence in the region. Pío Pico, California's last Mexican governor, allegedly acknowledged this in an 1846 speech before a military council:

> We find ourselves suddenly threatened by hordes of Yankee emigrants, who have already begun to flock into our country, and whose progress

we cannot arrest. Already have the wagons of that perfidious people scaled the almost inaccessible summits of the Sierra Nevada, crossed the entire continent, and penetrated the fruitful valley of the Sacramento. What that astonishing people will next undertake, I cannot say; but in whatever enterprise they embark they will be sure to prove successful. Already are these adventurous land-voyagers spreading themselves far and wide over a country which seems suited to their tastes. They are cultivating farms, establishing vineyards, erecting mills, sawing up lumber, building workshops, and doing a thousand other things which seem natural to them, but which Californians neglect or despise.

Despite some doubts over the authenticity of this statement, it nonetheless reflects a growing trend in California by the 1840s. In 1845 John L. O'Sullivan, editor of the *Democratic Review* and the *New York Morning News,* claimed that it was Americans' "manifest destiny to overspread the continent allotted by Providence for the free development of our yearly multiplying millions." Most Americans shared with O'Sullivan a desire to settle western territories and extend the boundaries of the United States to the Pacific Ocean. Proponents of this ideology argued that annexation of Mexico's northern provinces (which included the present-day states of California, Nevada, Utah, Arizona, New Mexico, and parts of Texas and Colorado) would facilitate economic growth and the spread of republican-style government. White supremacy, however, lay at the heart of Manifest Destiny. Anglo-Saxons believed themselves to be racially superior to Indians and Mexicans who inhabited the West. O'Sullivan and other annexationists believed that Mexicans were incapable of governing California and thus unfit to maintain possession of the territory:

California will, probably, next fall away from the loose adhesion which, in such a country as Mexico, holds a remote province in a slight equivocal kind of dependence on the metropolis. Imbecile and distracted, Mexico never can exert any real government authority over such a country....The Anglo-Saxon foot is already on [California's] borders. Already the advance guard of the irresistible army of Anglo-Saxon emigration has begun to pour down upon it, armed with the plough and the rifle, and marking its trail with schools and colleges, courts and representative halls, mills and meeting-houses. A population will soon be in actual occupation of California, over which it will be idle for Mexico to dream of dominion.

Currier & Ives, *The Way They Go to California*, ca. 1849. This Gold Rush cartoon shows how white settlers poured into California following the discovery of gold in 1848. Large-scale white settlement brought an end to the atmosphere of racial tolerance that characterized California during the Spanish and Mexican periods. Courtesy of the Library of Congress, LC-USZ62-104557.

THE WAY THEY GO TO CALIFORNIA.

Running for office in 1844, presidential candidate James K. Polk promised Americans that he would extend the boundaries of the United States by annexing Texas, which had declared its independence from Mexico in 1836. Shortly after taking office in 1845, Polk fulfilled his campaign pledge as Texas was added to the Union. But the annexation of Texas left open the question of the exact boundary between the United States and Mexico. Negotiations to resolve this issue collapsed as American diplomats—acting under orders from Polk—pressured Mexico to surrender not only the disputed territory but *all* of Mexico's northern territory. After the Mexican government rejected this proposal, Polk decided to abandon diplomacy in favor of aggression. In a deliberate attempt to provoke war with Mexico, Polk ordered U.S. troops into disputed territory south of the Nueces River. After several Mexican soldiers fired on what they considered an invading force of Americans, the U.S. officially declared war on Mexico.

The Mexican-American War endured for two years and ended with the signing of the Treaty of Guadalupe Hidalgo in 1848. The treaty ceded all of Mexico's northern provinces, including California, to the United States. The treaty, along with the discovery of gold that same year, led to the "actual occupation of California" by white settlers O'Sullivan had prophesied three years earlier. The Treaty of Guadalupe Hidalgo stated that "property of every kind" owned by Mexicans living in territories surrendered to the United States would be "inviolably respected." Most American settlers, however, believed that all land taken from Mexico now belonged to the United States by right of conquest. Furthermore, they rejected the idea that a few hundred

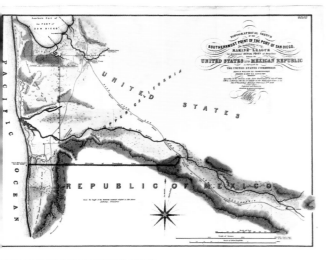

"Topographical Sketch of the Southern-most Point of the Port of San Diego and Measurement of the Marine League for Determining Initial Point of Boundary between the United States and Mexico as Surveyed by the United States Commission John B. Weller U.S. Commissioner, Andrew B. Gray U.S. Surveyor, agreeably to the decision of the Joint Commission of July 9th 1849, and in conformity with the 5th Article of the Treaty dated at the City of Guadalupe Hidalgo February 2nd 1848." Projected and Drawn by Andrew B. Gray, (Civil Engineer) U.S. Surveyor, copied by P. M. McGill C.E., Washington D.C., 1849. Courtesy of Coronado Public Library.

…eaty of Peace, Friendship, Limits …d Settlement between the United …ates of America and the Mexican …public (also known as the Treaty … Guadalupe Hidalgo), 1848. Cour-…sy of the Library of Congress.

Mexican ranchos could encompass some thirteen million acres of land in California. This along with official reports that challenged the legitimacy of most Mexican-era land grants encouraged white settlers to ignore Mexican land claims and "squat" on Mexican property.

To resolve the confusion over land ownership, Congress passed the California Land Act of 1851. The bill established a board of three commissioners to determine the validity of Mexican land titles. All rejected land claims would become public lands. Claimants who were denied by the commission could appeal in federal court and then the U.S. Supreme Court. If the courts upheld such claims, all settlers that had moved onto rancho lands would be forced to move. However, court proceedings often took many years and drained the finances of rancho owners. To raise money, many rancho owners either sold part or all of their lands to settlers. Other rancheros, meanwhile, would fall prey to unscrupulous American creditors who offered short-term mortgages with ridiculously high interest rates. Most Californios were accustomed to a more relaxed credit system and low interest rates that placed less pressure on the borrower. American bankers and lenders, however, demanded immediate repayment of debts and confiscated most

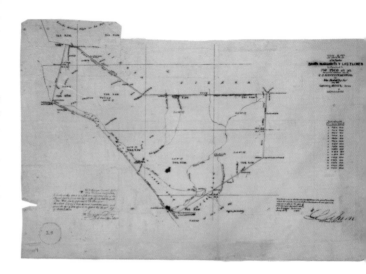

"Rancho Santa Margarita y Las Flores." In many ways, the story of this rancho reflects the plight of many Californios after the U.S. annexed California in 1848. For years, Pío Pico and his brother waged a costly legal battle to maintain ownership of the rancho, but on the brink of bankruptcy, Pico was eventually forced to sell it to his brother-in-law Juan Forster. This scenario occurred across California throughout the last half of the nineteenth century. Courtesy of The Bancroft Library, University of California, Land Case Maps Collection, Map E-1362A.

if not all the property of Californios who defaulted on their loans. These and other practices destroyed the old rancho elite.

Perhaps no two people represented the decline of the Californios more dramatically than Andrés and Pío Pico, both of whom had been at one time among the largest landowners of southern California. To secure credit, they mortgaged their Rancho Santa Margarita y Las Flores, located near Mission San Juan Capistrano, to two San Francisco lenders, Pioche and Bierque, for $44,000 with interest at 3 percent a month. They also mortgaged many of their properties around Los Angeles. Before long, the Picos defaulted on their loan payment and were forced to relinquish their huge rancho to Don Juan Forster. As his other properties transferred to other creditors, Pío Pico, like many of the other Californios, was reduced to poverty.

Besides losing their land and economic strength, Californios were placed at or near the bottom of the new social order. The period of racial tolerance that existed during Spanish and Mexican rule was over. Now, Anglo-American ideas of white supremacy and racial segregation permeated every aspect of California society.

Most Americans regarded Mexicans as culturally backward and racially inferior. Undoubtedly, many agreed with Thomas Jefferson Farnham, a white attorney from Illinois who, after settling in Monterey in 1841, concluded that "the Californians [Mexicans] are an imbecile, pusillanimous race of men, and unfit to control the destinies of that beautiful country." Writing in the 1850s, Charlie E. Huse, a white settler, described Mexicans in Santa Barbara as the "dregs of society…The greatest part of the [Mexican] population is lazy, does not work, does not pay its debts, does not keep its word, is full of envy, of ill will, of cunning, craft and fraud, falsehood and ignorance." Huse's and Farnham's attitude reflected that of a growing number of Anglo settlers in California whose Protestant upbringing and anti-Catholic views contributed to the atmosphere of racial intolerance and nativism that swept through the state. Santa Barbara, Los Angeles, and other California towns became hotbeds of racial violence. William Streeter, a Santa Barbara resident, attributed the widespread violence to the post–Gold Rush "influx of rough characters." These newcomers "exposed the simple Californians [Mexicans] to many dangers, not to speak of the ill treatment and the advantage taken of their simplicity…The majority of these rough, reckless men had little respect for the persons or property of the Californians. The generous hospitality of the latter was often repaid with insult…This treatment embittered them towards the Americans and together with other causes prevented their reconciliation to the American occupation."

During the Spanish and Mexican periods of California's history, race had not played a central role in determining one's social rank. But with the American takeover of California, laws were quickly adopted that took away from Mexicans, Asians, African Americans, and Native Americans their civil rights.

THE BANDITS BRIDE.

Henry R. Robinson, *The Bandit's Bride,* May 5, 1847. This editorial cartoon, published during the Mexican-American War in the *New York Herald,* which depicts a woman being abducted by Mexican bandits, reflects increasing anti-Mexican sentiment in the U.S. Courtesy of the Library of Congress, LC-USZ62-62675.

The California state legislature, for instance, passed ordinances that excluded Mexicans and Asians from mining districts. In 1850 the California legislature created a tax which required miners who were not U.S. citizens to pay a fee of twenty dollars a month, well beyond the reach of most Mexicans and Asians. Individuals who refused to comply with this law were barred from mining. Thousands of Mexicans, including many who were U.S. citizens, were driven from the mines.

The California constitution of 1849 represents the formal close of the era of racial tolerance in California. Despite some protests from Mexican-American and white delegates, the convention voted to disfranchise "Indians, Africans, and descendants of Africans." Ironically, at least one of the delegates, Antonio María Pico, had African heritage, but he apparently did not voice any opposition to this vote. Other discriminatory measures soon followed. The 1849-50 state legislature limited membership in the state militia to "free white males," prohibited nonwhite testimony in court cases involving whites, and adopted "vagrancy" laws that created a system of Indian slavery that remained in effect until after the end of the Civil War. Throughout the 1850s the state legislature voted to allow anyone who claimed them as ex-slaves to detain blacks who had entered the state before 1850, while denying blacks the right to testify on their behalf. Finally, the legislature unsuccessfully attempted to set up a "coolie" labor system using Asian labor.

Indeed, much had changed in California from the time of Anza's arrival to the transfer of California to the United States. It began as a place that afforded Afro-Latinos like the Tapias and the Picos the opportunity to transition from poverty to prosperity—to have title to thousands of acres of land, exercise political power, and be treated with respect. The vast majority of African Americans in the United States, meanwhile, still languished in chattel slavery. California had been a remarkably diverse and vibrant community where people of different races and ethnicities lived and worked together. Above all, it was a place where "race" did not function as an impediment to social, political, and economic advancement. What does this history mean to us today? From the end of the Mexican era to the present, Californians have been struggling with the demon of racism. With outrages against American Indians and Americans of African, Asian, or Mexican descent, or anyone else identified by the white population as "other," the damage and pain inflicted by racism have been crippling, not only to the victims but to the perpetrators. A cynical view is that racism has always been with us, built into the human condition and a constant throughout history. Nothing could be further from the truth, as this study of pre–Gold Rush California has shown us.

Although it is not generally apparent from paintings and other depictions of early California, many members of the pioneering Anza expeditions and Spanish California's most prominent families were of mixed race—Hispanic, Indian, and African. At a time when slavery was still legal in the United States, these Afro-Latinos made major contributions to early California. They were landowners, soldiers, judges, governors, and patriarchs of some of the state's most influential families. They opened up trails, led rebellions, and established ranchos and pueblos that would become the basis for many of today's cities.

This pamphlet provides an overview of these remarkable families, describes their backgrounds, and investigates the ways in which they reshaped early California. It also provides us with an image of a society in which the relationships between races, and racism itself, were far different, and perhaps less rigidly understood, than they are today.

Damany Fisher, a native of Sacramento, received his Ph.D. from the University of California, Berkeley. He currently teaches American history at Mt. San Antonio College in Walnut, California. *Author photo by James Fisher*

Copublished with the Juan Bautista de Anza National Historic Trail, National Park Service

ISBN 978-1-59714-145-1

HEYDAY